Precious Life

By Biba Ghaifan

Giant Publishing Company
Lincoln, Nebraska, USA

2021 by Biba Ghaifan

Published by Giant Publishing Company
Post Office Box 6455
Lincoln, NE 68506
www.giantpublishingcompany.com

Printed in the United States of America

Cover image courtesy of pexels.com
Author photo by Niet Tuom

ISBN: 978-1-7352827-2-5

To my wonderful, amazing, spiritual parents.
Thank you for believing in me, and inspiring me.
I love you both.

Listing of poems

Gift of Life.....................................Page 1
The Journey....................................Page 2
Journey with God.............................Page 3
The Path of Faith.............................Page 4
Life with Jesus................................Page 5
Who Am I......................................Page 6
The Identity...................................Page 7
I AM...Page 9
My Best Friend, JC...........................Page 10
Thank You.....................................Page 11
ABC Jesus.....................................Page 13
Fight...Page 15
Trust Him......................................Page 16
This Too Shall Pass...........................Page 17
Friend of Jesus................................Page 18
Friendship.....................................Page 20
Unconditional Love...........................Page 21
Thankful.......................................Page 23
My Child.......................................Page 25
Little Souls....................................Page 26
Gift of Jesus...................................Page 27
A True Hero...................................Page 28
Words from J.E.S.U.S.........................Page 29
In Your Presence..............................Page 30
Rest..Page 31
True Parenthood...............................Page 32
Spiritual Covering.............................Page 34
Welcome Home................................Page 36
I LOVE YOU...................................Page 39
Wait for Your Time............................Page 41

Listing of poems, continued

Enjoy the Season............................Page 43
Beauty.......................................Page 45
Child's Faith................................Page 47
Letter from Jesus...........................Page 48
WORD..Page 50
Special Grace...............................Page 51
His Hand....................................Page 53
Spiritual Father............................Page 55
Spiritual Mother............................Page 58
Thanksgiving Praise.........................Page 60
Sisterhood..................................Page 62
Sweet Lady..................................Page 64
Armor of God................................Page 66
Encouraging Words...........................Page 68
Reunite with Love...........................Page 70
The Healer..................................Page 71
Philippians 4:13............................Page 73
Smile.......................................Page 75
No-Limits...................................Page 77
Prince of Peace.............................Page 79
Child's Birth...............................Page 80
Dial 333....................................Page 82
Galatian Fruits.............................Page 83
Happy Birthday Jesus........................Page 85
College.....................................Page 86
May 9, 2020.................................Page 87
For Her.....................................Page 88
Through the Storms..........................Page 89
Butterfly...................................Page 92
Resurrection................................Page 93

Foreword

I met Biba Ghaifan in the spring of 2015, and I can personally attest to the amazing transformation that has occurred in her life. Biba received Jesus Christ as her savior shortly after she began attending No-Limits International Christian Center in Lincoln, Nebraska. The Lord took a young girl who had been hurt by many, and transformed her into a confident, strong, and beautiful young woman. Like a caterpillar emerging from a cocoon as a beautiful butterfly, Biba emerged from a shell of hurt and distrust, and transformed before our very eyes into the servant of God that He always intended her to be.

I am blessed to know Biba and to count her as my friend. You will be blessed by this collection of her beautiful poetry.

Julie Anshasi – 2021 Illumination Book Awards Silver Medal winner

Gift of Life

Life is a precious gift
A gift given by God
Life is a journey that leads you
Into becoming you
It helps you find your purpose
It helps you find your identity
The identity of Christ is within you
That helps you find your true purpose

Life brings you hurdles
So jump over it
It brings you lemons
So make lemonade

Every moment of life is beautiful
Rather good or bad
Life is still beautiful
Cherish your loved ones
Inspire others
Love yourself
Love others
Be grateful
Be thankful
Enjoy the moment
Live the moment
The gift of life
Is truly a blessing

The word life stands for
"Live It Fully Everyday"

1

The Journey

I walk this journey
It's a long journey
But I am not alone

This journey is led
By someone special
He is the leader
Every step, He takes
I also take mine
One step at a time

There will be challenges
Along this journey
But with Him
We'll overcome it

The journey with Jesus
Isn't an easy one
But His word says
"He will never leave you,
Nor forsake you"

So hold on to Him
Believe in Him
Follow Him

Because this journey is worth going for
Let's walk this beautiful journey
With our friend, Jesus

Journey with God

This journey with God
Isn't easy
But with God
It will be easy
We walk by faith
Not by sight
Enemies come from all directions
But God is in all directions

My deliverer
My protector
My Healer
There's no one greater
Than the one above

Stones are thrown
From left to right
But I say back to sender
When God blesses
No man can stop it

Haters will hate
But I will appreciate
Just don't hate
Come and rejoice
With those who rejoice

The Path of Faith

I am going on a path,
A path that leads
To the evidence, assurance of
Things hope for that are not seen

This path is known to every human race
It's within their hearts
Its within their inner souls

This path makes you believe
This path gives you confidence
This path drives out fear
This path brings you hope

It's a beautiful path
It's an amazing path
This is a true path
The one and only path
That leads you to your destiny

You are not walking alone
There is someone with you
He is your leader
He leads, you follow

I love this beautiful path
Some call it "taking a risk"
I call it "the path of faith"

4

Life with Jesus

I once was a lost girl
But now I've been found
Life has its ups and downs
Like a roller coaster
You might never know
When you'll fall
Nor when you'll rise
Always expect the good and bad
I always thought
I had the good life
Until Jesus came through
He was always there
Through thick and thin
My life has been formed
Better than ever before
All because of Jesus
The true creator of life
The journey with Him
Isn't easy but worth it
Don't lose hope
Don't lose sight
But focus on Him
And you'll see Him
My life right now
Is a purposeful life
A life I want to continue pursing with Jesus
Life with Jesus is truly worth living

Who Am I?

Who am I?
I am…
What am I…?
I am...

I am a child of God
Created by Him
Defined by Him
My identity is within Him

I am beautiful
Beautiful are His works
Everything He created is good
The creation is beautiful as I am

I am strong
I am courageous
I am an overcomer

Challenges may come, but I'll overcome them
Storms may come, but I'll stand strong through
them

I am victorious
I am brave
I am bold

I am who God says I am
Because the "I am"
Is within me

The Identity

Identity is you
Identity is the inner you
Don't be afraid
To become you
You create you

It is enduring and changing
It's a source of expectations
But also, motivations
What makes you, is you

It is personal
But also, relational
People see you differently
Than how you see yourself
But that shouldn't stop you
From knowing you

Spend time on yourself
Get to know yourself
Don't depend on others
Cause they won't be there long
But depend on the one
That created you

Some may label you
Some may create you
But deep inside know who you are

Let us find our true identity

Not what society is defining us
Be the next generation to make an impact
You are your own voice
Speak out of your heart not fear
Stay true to yourself

Create a culture of you
A culture with
Your own beliefs
Your own values
Your own norms
Create the importance
Within you

Many cultures are around us
Many are created by us
Culture is within the group
Be the leader
That brings the group

It's not about the race or color
We're all created differently
To bring unity to the nation
To bring peace to the nation
Let us come in love not hate
Love drives out hate
Remember the pledge
One nation under God
So let us be a true nation

I AM

Who are you?
Others may say
Who am I?
You may say

I am who God says I am
I am what God says I am
I am where God says I am

I am loved
Because He first loved me
I am beautiful
Because He created me
I am blessed
Because He blessed me

I am not what others say
I am not what others think
I am not what others label

I know who I am
I know who I belong to
I know who chose me
The I am is who I am

Know your value
Know your worth
Know your standard
Know who you are
Because the I am is with you

My Best Friend, JC

My one and only friend
That I could trust and I know
Wouldn't be fake nor pretend

Day and night, He always listens
To my prayers and I know
He will always be my friend

No matter what. I am a Christian
That wants to learn and flow
In His presence. Where I can spend

My life in heaven. He has a vision
For me. I keep my head high and not low.
I will always love my amazing friend.

The past is gone and I made a decision
To follow Him. I made a mistake, He says no,
And try again. He cleansed me and will send

Me to many nations. Together, we have a mission
To conquer the world. I do believe that I will go
To make a difference with my true friend.
I will always and forever love you till the very end.

Thank You

Oh God, I thank you
For watching me daily
Even when I fall
Your hands reach out to me

Oh God, I thank you
For protecting me daily
Even when troubles come
You are still there

Oh God, I thank you
For loving me daily
Even when I have nothing
You are the one I need

Oh God, I thank you
For blessing me daily
Even when I don't deserve
But your grace is sufficient for me

Oh God, I thank you
For giving me breath daily
That I am able to see
And grow in your ways

Oh God, I thank you
For being my friend daily
And never leaving me

Oh God, I thank you

For being my father
And I am your child
Because without you
I am nothing.

ABC Jesus

My God is ......

Alpha and Omega

Beautiful are His works

Creator of heaven and earth

Dominion of the entire world

Everlasting blessings

Flowing within us

Glory, Glory to our

Heavenly Father

Incredible, He is

Jesus is the name

King of Kings

Lamb that was slain

Marvelous are His wonders

Never left us nor forsaken us

Omnipotent, who is all

Powerful and supreme

Quick to forgive us

Righteousness, He is

Savior of all,

The entire

Universe will bow down

Very soon and will

Worship Him

X leads to

Your knees, saying Yahweh of Mount

Zion

Fight

Let's fight
The fight of faith

Let's win
Let's win this fight

Together,
We're stronger
Together,
We're overcomers

The fight to victory
The fight to freedom
The fight to breakthrough
Is the fight we declare

You're not alone
God is with us
He will fight
For you and me

Stay strong
Have faith
Keep fighting
We will win
This fight of faith

Trust Him

When life seems useless
No direction
No guidance
I put my trust in Him

When everyone accused me as guilty
But I had no guilt in me
I looked up to Him
Because I trust Him

When problems come after another
Trying to find solutions
But nowhere to start
I put my trust in Him

When hope seems to disappear
My faith starts to fade
It's the world and I
Fighting one another

A small voice whispers
"Keep strong, my child"
Then I know I am not alone
I had put my trust in Him

Because trusting Him is all I could do

This Too Shall Pass

There are moments of troubles
There are moments of struggles
You're trying to stay strong
But there's no strength
Where do I look?
Where do I turn?
Heard a voice within me
Like an angel speaking to me
"This too shall pass"
What does this mean…
Lift your head up
Wipe your tears
Walk with power
Walk with authority
This storm shall pass

Friend of Jesus

Someone who cares
Someone who shares
Someone who gives

A friend of Jesus,
Is a friend indeed

Someone ready to listen
Someone ready to give a hand
Someone ready to help you

A friend of Jesus,
Is a friend indeed

Someone that corrects
When you're wrong
Without judging you
But still loving you

In the darkest moments
When no one to turn to
When hope seems lost
That someone is there

Someone who admires
Someone who loves
Someone who adores

A person that thinks about you
A person that protects you
A person that fights for you

This someone is a friend of Jesus,
Who is a friend, indeed
Let us be a friend of Jesus

Friendship

There are many friends
But you're a different friend
A friend of Jesus
Is a friend indeed

Gentle
Love
Kind
Speaks of you

Laughter is our medicine
Joy is our strength
Time together
Enjoying each other
Humor is our name
Sharing moments
Sharing stories

A friend like you
Is what I need
A true friend of Jesus
Is a true friend of mine

Unconditional Love

Love is sharing
Love is caring
Love is loving

When everyone leaves
You're all alone but
Love is there

Love drives out fear
Love drives out hate
Love drives out guilt

Love is patient
Love is kind
Love is peace

When you make a mistake
Love is there
When you sin
Love is there
When you cry
Love is there

This love is here
This love is for you and me
This love is everywhere

This love adores
This love admires
This love amazes

When you're in trouble
Love protects
When you're down
Love lifts you up

This is the true love
The unconditional love

This love is Jesus

Thankful

A day of thanksgiving
Is a day of giving thanks
When I was lost,
He found me
When I was hopeless
He gave me hope

When I felt like nobody -
Because of Him,
I am somebody
Because of Him,
I am alive
Because of Him,
I am loved

A love that is unconditional
A love that dwells within my heart
A love that's irreplaceable
Because of Him,
Love is birthed
Within me

Thank you for the love that I could share with the
world of your goodness.

A day to celebrate
A day to give thanks

Thank you for the blessings
Thank you for the healings
Thank you for the miracles
Thank you for the breakthrough

We make mistakes
But you still take us

For every season
There is a time
But this day is the day
We say thank you,

Thank you for all you have done,
Thank you for all you have provided
Your love for us is amazing
It can't be compared to anyone

My Child

A child is precious in God's sight
Those called by God
Are children of God

Children are a gift from God
He is your heavenly father
He has a purpose for you
He is taking care of you

My child, rise I am here
My child, I am your protector
My child, be brave and bold

No weapon formed against you shall prosper
I am the creator of the universe
I formed you in your mother's womb
Don't worry about anything
Lift your head up high

I am here for you
I will save you
I will watch over you

I am your Father
You are My Child

Little Souls

Every day, I wake up
Just for a beautiful soul
The little souls
So innocent in God's eyes
But guilty in human eyes
I thank God
For a heart like mine
Because my heart
Adores the little souls
Some days are good
Some days are bad
But my heart
Remains the same
For these beautiful souls
I love to teach them
The word of God
That will dwell within
Their little hearts
I know they are safe
In my Father's hands
My desire is for these little souls
To grow and love
The ways of God
Because God truly adores them
Just like I do
God bless these little souls

Gift of Jesus

A joyful day -
To celebrate today.
A new born baby
Lying on the hay

Coming to bring unity
For the whole nation,
By dying and bringing salvation.

Laid in a manger
To one day become a King.
Glory, glory to our King

A true hero given unto us
To bring love, peace, and hope
This is the true gift for us
That is with us every day,
Held in our little hearts
That we carry daily.

There is no other greater
Gift than the gift -
Of baby
Jesus

A True Hero

My hero,
My only hero
He is my Father
He is my King
He has done so much for me
He might not wear a cape
But He can truly save the world
Only those that need help
He will save them
I feel His presence daily
I feel His love daily

He is my motivation
He is my inspiration
He is my salvation

I call upon Him
Because I need Him
He can be your hero too

My hero,
My true hero
Thank you for saving me
Thank you for being there for me

#JesusSaves

Words from J.E.S.U.S

Just believe in my words

Every word spoken by me will come to pass

Say the word, watch the work

Until you believe and have faith in me, I will do the impossible

Speak the word into existence

"In the beginning the Word already existed; the Word was with God, and the Word was God. From the very beginning the Word was with God. Through Him God made all things; not one thing in all creation was made without Him. The Word was the source of life, and this life brought light to humanity."
(John 1:1-4, GNB)

In Your Presence

I've been to a place
Where there is peace
No one understands you
But only you

Trouble comes like a wind
Fades away like the clouds

I laugh, cry, and smile
Because I am
In your presence

Angels surrounded
Atmosphere changes
Where I express myself
Where I scream and shout
FREEDOM!

The warm feeling
Of the touch of God
Erasing my sins
Renewing my mind

Being myself
In His presence
No judgment
No worries
Just a feeling
I call home

Rest

When life troubles you
No strength to carry on
Finding ways to escape
Mind full of endless thoughts

Let's cast those burdens
Let's remove the loads
Shake it off your shoulders
Sweep it off your feet

Give it to Jesus
Lean on Jesus
Rest on Jesus
Take His yoke

He'll give you rest
Rest from troubles
Rest from struggles
Rest from thoughts

For He is
Gentle
Caring
Loving
Humble in heart

Matthew 11:28-30

True Parenthood

My parents,
My spiritual parents
I love you so much
I was brought to earth
By natural parents
But I've been raised
By spiritual parents

October 18,
Is the day God knew
I would manifest on earth
"Jeremiah 29:11"
My Mama, My Papa
Raised me into someone
I never thought existed

You gave birth to the real me
The sweetheart,
The teacher,
The graduate,

A beautiful lady,
A talented lady,
A creative lady,

A lady who would inspire others
A lady who would motivate others
A lady who would encourage others

In my crying stages,
You wiped my tears
In my hopeless moments
You gave me hope
In my mistakes,
You corrected me,
While loving me,
Without judging me

When I felt unloved,
You showed me love
When I thought I was nobody
You made me into somebody

Thank you for being there
In the bad times
In the good times
And for every moment

Thank you for raising me as your own child

Thank you, Papa, for choosing Mama
Thank you, Mama, for saying "I DO"

Dedicated to my wonderful spiritual parents

Spiritual Covering

A man with authority
A woman with divine inspiration
A man who upholds power
A woman with respect

Both are anointed, chosen by God

A man who is generous
A woman who is gentle
A man full of charm
A woman full of glamour

You teach us the word of God and show us your
love that God gave you.
You carry the principles of God, giving an
authority to change nations for the glory of God.

A man of compassion
A woman with love

They are faithful, determined, and loyal to God

A man who is a leader
A woman who is a helper
A mother of nations
A father of faith

They are truly a blessing; because of them, we are blessed.
A gift from God given unto us, revealing the visions and dreams of God's people.

They are humble, obedient, and undefeated.

An Apostle with bulldozer anointing
The Prophetic eye, seer of God

Welcome Home

Once a lost girl roaming the streets
Looking for a place to call home
I've been welcomed to a home
But it didn't feel like a home

In that home, I was judged
In that home, I was mistreated
In that home, I felt lonely
In that home, I felt depressed
No one to trust
No one to talk to
No one to call my friend

Time passed by,
Still didn't feel like I belonged there
Instead of them helping
They had accused me
I felt like the world didn't need me
I felt like they didn't need me
Thinking of ending my life
Thinking of disappearing forever
There is no life here

So running away
Running far, far away
Searching for a new home
A home where I belong
A home full of love

A home full of peace
A home that is truly a home

Time passed by,
I finally reached a place
It was different
It was unique
It was beautiful

As I stepped inside,
I felt my heart with joy
I felt my spirit with peace
I felt butterflies in my tummy
I felt a breeze within me
I felt a love that is unexplainable
It's like a rebirth within me
It's like my life resurrected
Shame left me
Pain left me
Hate left me

This is the place
The place full of love
The place full of joy
The place full of peace
A small whisper said
"Welcome home"

Finally, I am home
A home for me

A home where I belong
A home where I am needed
A home with no judgment
A home with a pure heart
A home called NICC
Truly, this is my home

NICC – No-Limits International Christian Center

I LOVE YOU

I love you
My child
My precious one
My golden star

I was there with you
I am here with you
When no one was there
I was watching you
Through everything
I still love you

I know your past
I know your present
I know your future
I still love you

Even when you're far
I protected you
Even through trials
I saved you
But I still love you

It was my love
It was my mercy
It was my grace
I still love you

Because of me
You're alive
You're here
I will love you

I need you
I want you
You are mine

Because I LOVE YOU

Wait For Your Time

Patience is the key
Patience will last
Patience brings joy

The word wait means being patient,
Means the right time

Time comes in various ways,
Time could be now, later, or soon
Time could be days, weeks, or months
Time could be year, next year, or years

But if it's God's timing
Then wait upon Him
He wouldn't disappoint you
He protects you
Because He knows you

There's a time for everything
A time for healing
A time for graduating
A time for birthing
A time for building
"Ecclesiastes 3:1-8"

Don't look at others' time
But wait for your time
Your time is the perfect time

Your time is precious

Your time brings
Victorious
Blessings,
Celebrations

A wise person said,
"If you rush, you crash."

If God says wait
Then wait,
If God says it's time
Then it's time
Wait for God's time
Which will be your time

Enjoy the Season

This world is set on time
Ages go up
Trends change
People come and go
People live and die
Things happen for a reason
So why not enjoy the season
Let's look around us
Look around you
There's a time for everything
There's a time for seasons
Just like every holiday
Comes with its season
Comes with its month

Let's enjoy the season
Let's live the season
There's a purpose to it
There's a beauty of it
Enjoy the blessings
Enjoy the friendships
Spend time with family
Encourage others
Help each other

Life is too precious
Enjoy the now
Before it's all gone

Be present
Be in the moment
Live.
Laugh.
Love.

This is the season
This is the time
Enjoy it
Live it

This season will pass
It will be a history
A history to the unknown
Enjoy it while you can
A clock doesn't stop
So move with it
Let's enjoy the season

Beauty

What is beauty?
Beauty is defined by
Your values
Your character
Your surroundings

Beauty is life
Life is beautiful
You are beautiful
The beauty of nature
The beauty of life
Brings happiness
Brings peace
Brings freedom

You create the beauty
Even in the storms
There's beauty within
Through troubles
Through struggles
You create the beauty of peace
The peace in your soul
The peace around you
Those challenges won't be there long
Look forward to something special

You are special
You are unique

The Beautifier created you
The Creator made you beautiful
Your flaws make you beautiful
He made the world beautiful
Beautiful are His works
There's a beauty within you
The inner beauty
The outer beauty
Embrace the beauty
Love the beauty
Enjoy the moment because
The world is full of beauty

Child's Faith

Be like a child
A child of faith
Who is a free spirit
No worries
No fears
Ready for an adventure
Always expects the best
Always looking forward
Waiting for the parents' promises
Not knowing how it's going to happen
But always ready to receive

The circumstances don't matter
A child knows the promise will come
The promise will be fulfilled

The child had crazy faith
The child always believed
The child asked so
The child will receive

We are that child
A child of God
A child with faith
A child that believed
God's promises will be fulfilled

Letter From Jesus

Dear Beloved Child,

I am with you
I am always here
Every moment
Every memory

I never left your side
Have you left mine?
Either way, I am here to stay
Stay with you in everything

I am the shoulder to cry on
I am the hand to help you
Believe in me
Trust in me

Don't worry about everything
I will change the impossible to possible

You are my own
My precious, my jewel
Life could be troubling
I'll protect you
I'll shield you
No weapon formed against you shall prosper

Hold my hand
Come to me
I love you
Always and forever

Love, Your Heavenly Father

WORD

I am what you say
I am what you bring
I am the word
The words of life
The words of death
Speak life
I manifest life
Speak death
I manifest death
Kind words are sweet
Sweet for your soul
Sweet for your body
Proverbs 18:4

I am the tool
I am the force
I bring power within you
I change the atmosphere for you
Be careful little tongue
Choose victory or
Choose destruction
Think before you speak
You are what you say
Use me wisely
Use me carefully
I am the word
Proverbs 18:21

Special Grace

The grace of God is sufficient

Living my desires
Pursuing my desires
But deep down
I felt empty
I felt lonely
I felt depressed
Not caring about others
Not caring about the world
Not caring about life
Only to think about my selfish desires
People say Jesus exists
Yes, of course He exists
But your actions don't exist

Then one day,
A special Grace
The grace of God
Came through like never before
The glory reflected upon a vessel
A vessel ready to be used
A vessel for the kingdom of God
A vessel that proves action that Jesus exists
This vessel spoke to my inner man
The hidden man,
The soul and spirit
Took away my shame

Took away my desires
Took away my pain

It is truly the grace of God
A special Grace
Who became
My special friend,
My special sister

I thank God for this special vessel
Because the grace of God is sufficient

His Hand

Need a hand
A helping hand
The hand of God
To pull you up

His hand is there
Reach up and grab it
His hand is powerful
Speak and declare it

When we hear His voice
When we obey Him
He gives us His hand
And we give to others

His hand working through me
His hand working through you
You need a hand
I need a hand

His hand comforts
His hand heals
His hand delivers

His hand is
Gentle
Kind
Sweet

Loving

Don't fear
His hand helps
Through it all
Reach out
Grab it

You are safe
With His hand

The hand of God

Spiritual Father

Today is the day
We celebrate
A special person

He is the father
A father to sons
A father of faith
A father to nations

Who is acclaimed by God
Chosen for me
To change my life
To rebirth my life
Into a purposeful life

A man from far away
A man of God
A man that
Changed my life

Today, I am somebody
Because of this man

This special man
Brings words of
Wisdom
Knowledge
Understanding

My life is redeemed
Because of him
The blessings I have
Are because of him
The favor I have
Is because of him

The unconditional love
It's the love of Jesus
That brings life
That brings joy
That brings peace
Into my life

He wants the best for me
He protects me
He encourages me

He has done so much for me
In everything
He has taken me as his own

I am grateful
I am honored
I am blessed
To be his

Always there
Always listens

Always shares
Always loves

A prayerful father
A forgiving father
A loving father

Faithfulness
Compassion
Dedication
Speak of him

Truly called
The anointed
Holy Spirit-filled
Chosen one
For God's people

He is the Apostle
The Bulldozer
My True Father
But mostly
My special Father

Spiritual Mother

A beautiful woman
Full of love,
Very gentle
Loves conditionally
Always caring,
Protecting,
And cherishing everyone

A mother of all nations
But a special mother to me
Always wants the best for me

You guided me
You dressed me
You cared for me
Even in my stubbornness
You loved me

When I made a mistake
You corrected me
You never left my side
Always there to give a hand

Without you,
I wouldn't find my identity

A beautiful flower has
Been given unto me
Someone with care
And with love
No words can describe
How amazing she is

When I fall, she's there
When I rise, she's there

It's like a God-given gift unto me
That is irreplaceable
Only the Lord could bring it
Forth for the right time

She loves me with unconditional love
She uplifts me
She wipes my tears
She cares
She shares
She holds my hand
Like mother and daughter

Thanksgiving Praise

Every day
Is a thankful day
A day to remember Him
A day to give thanks
A day to be grateful
Tomorrow isn't promised

In the storms,
I'll praise Him
In the good times,
I'll praise Him
Through the pain
I'll praise Him
Through the struggles,
I'll praise Him

I am thankful for every moment
Because He is there in every moment
I am thankful for His blessings
I am thankful for His protection
I am thankful for His presence

Because without Him
I wouldn't be here
When I look around
I am thankful for His creation
When I see my spiritual parents
I am thankful for them

The people He placed in my life
Either for blessings or lessons
I am thankful for them

The love He shows me every day
I am truly grateful
It's the unconditional love

That cares for me
That protects me
That loves me
That sees me
For who I am

Without this love
I wouldn't love myself
But I know I am created
Beautifully
Wonderfully
In His image

So I am thankful and grateful
Thank you, Lord, for everything

Sisterhood

We are friends
We are sisters
We are family

Together,
We are stronger
Together,
We are courageous
Together,
We are unstoppable

Lifting one another
Motiving one another
Inspiring one another
Praying for one another

Honesty
Loyalty
Unity
Speaks of us

Anointed
Chosen
Called
For His glory

We are …
Loved

Redeemed
Favored
Overcomers
Happy

We are the Crown Jewels

Sweet Lady

A sweet soul
A sweet lady
Such a beauty
In her inner soul

Her words are
Sweet and genuine
Full of wisdom
Full of knowledge

She's unique
She's special
She's a vessel
Chosen vessel

Admired by God
Loved by her Father
Inspiration to others
Leader for nations
Called and chosen

This sweet lady
This sweet soul
This sweet vessel

I admire her
I adore her
She's my mentor

My inspiration
My leader
My motivator

Dedicated to Sister Julie

Armor of God

Child of God
Let go
Let God

Don't fight alone
Let Him fight for you
Give Him the battle
He will do it for you
For you, alone

Let's stand firm
Let's stand strong
Let's stand together

Watch Him win
Watch Him conquer
Watch Him defeat
Putting your enemies to shame

Put on the armor of God
Dress like a warrior
Dress like a winner
The battle has begun

Buckle up with the belt of Truth
Put on breastplate of Righteousness
Slip those shoes on for the gospel of Peace
Hold on to the shield of Faith

Cover your Head with the Helmet of Salvation
Finally, lift up the sword of the Spirit
Which bringeth the Word of God

Once again,
Child of God
Let go
Let God

No need to fight alone
Let Him fight for you
He will do the fight for you
For you, alone

Be courageous
Be strong
Be victorious

Ephesians 6: 10-18

Encouraging Words

Watch your words
They can be life or death
Choose life
So that you may live

Watch your words
Speak life to others
Create life in others
Create life for you

Words of life
Bringeth
Peace
Comfort
Love

Use your words
To build others
To create others
To motivate others

Speak kind
Speak gentle
Speak love

Others need your words
Others wait for your words
Others embrace your words

Let's use our words
To speak positive
To speak life
To speak love

Don't listen to the devil
His words are lies
He says you can't make it
But God says you can

God spoke life
And the world was created
God spoke life
And we were born

Remember His words
The words of life
Speak life to others
Speak life to yourself

Reunite with Love

It's about the love
Not the color or race
We're all created from one man
The one and only
Jesus Christ
So why hate
Just appreciate

This life is important
Because we represent
Our image for the next generation
This is our land, our nation

Through my eyes
I see a beautiful world
People of all races and colors
Coming together to reunite
Learning to love and reunite
Bringing our country in peace
Remember the pledge
One nation, under God
So let us be a true nation

The Healer

Miracles.
Signs.
Wonders.

The world brings pain
But God brings gain
Don't condemn yourself
Look at the Creator
He made you wonderful
He made you to be great

When pain strikes
He is your healer
Through bad relationships
He will heal you
Through the storms
He'll deliver you
Through the suffering
He will watch over you
In the crying moments
He wipes your tears
No matter what situation
He will be there
From the outer pain
To the inner pain
He'll heal all of you

You shall overcome this pain

By His stripes
You are healed
It's only a test
Into a testimony
Ask for the healing
The healer will answer

Philippians 4:13

"I can do all things through Christ who strengthens me."

Everything in this world is for you
Everything God created is for you
What you want to be
Is what you'll become
You can do all things
You can do everything

Becoming rich
Then be rich
Wanting degrees
Then get educated
Becoming CEO
Create businesses

Learn the skills of life
Learn to be successful
Learn the system of life

Ask for wisdom
Ask for creativity
Ask for innovation

He said, "Ask and you shall receive."
Why not ask for the impossible?
He is the God of possible

Don't limit Him
Don't limit yourself
Build a legacy
Build a brand
A brand that never existed
Something unique
Something different
Create the impossible to possible

Remember Philippians 4:13
"I can do all things through Christ who strengthens me."

Smile

Smile
The world needs you
Be strong
Don't let others pull you down
You are stronger than you think

Smile
It brightens the world
It motivates others
It brings healing

Smile
It's a beautiful thing
It's a characteristic
Developed within you

Smile
Through the storms
It is your peace
It is your strength

Smile
Someone is looking for it
Someone is watching you
Everything will be all right

Smile
It is what makes you
It is your beauty
It creates you

Smile for you

No-Limits

The heaven and the earth
Are created by Him
Within seven days
Everything was good

Even human beings
Were created by Him
Filled with many skills
Developed within them

One human being
Could become many things
In one body
You are a
Teacher, student, parent
Nurse, daughter, CEO
In human flesh

How could it possibly be?
The one Creator created this?
So why limit Him?

Everything you want
It is possible
Everything you want to be
It is possible

Go above your imagination
Go above the clouds
Look for the impossible
Look for the best

Become more than what you are

Go higher
Go bigger
We are born
To do greater things
We're here to dominate
Let's take charge
We are UNLIMITED

Prince of Peace

I've met a Prince
One of a kind
Who I trusted
Who I respected
Who I admired

He inspired me
He nurtured me
He adored me

He's a special Prince
His love is amazing
He gives me joy
He gives me peace

He is my knight in shining armor
He comforts me in times of trouble
He protects me in everything

When I call, He answers
When I am down, He uplifts me
He is my motivation
He is my inspiration

He is my Prince
I am His Princess

Child's Birth

What a day
A special day
To celebrate the birth
Of a beautiful baby
Of a handsome baby

The angels rejoice
The parents rejoice
The earth welcomes
Such a beautiful soul
That has been birthed

The heavenly father knows this day
The mother rejoices to see
Such a beautiful angel
In the palms of her hands
Nine months in the womb
But now held in her hands

Their love is irreplaceable
The child is bright
The future is bright
We pray for protection
Hand it to the heavens
For every child is a
Gift unto God
Let heaven rejoice

Let earth rejoice
We celebrate with you
Happy birthday

Dial 333

"Call to me, I will answer you"

When you need a friend
Someone to talk to
Someone to spend time with
Dial 333

Things are getting worse
Bills piling like mountains
Need financial assistance
Dial 333

Your body is aching
Looking for a doctor
A place for Healing
Dial 333

Need guidance
Looking for directions
Needing advice
Dial 333

Looking for answers
Pull out the Bible
Jeremiah 33:3
God will answer you

Galatian Fruits

A sweet taste to your soul
A sweet taste for you
The Word of God is sweet
Which bears the sweetest fruits

The fruit of LOVE
Brings bonds within you
Creates the beauty of you
1 Corinthians 13:1

The fruit of PEACE
Brings your soul to rest
When there's trouble
John 14:27

The fruit of JOY
Is like a river
Flowing with gladness
Proverbs 16:20

The fruit of PATIENCE
Brings the ability to wait
Upon the greatest desires
Without rushing through
Isaiah 40:31

The fruit of FAITHFULNESS
Brings trust

Brings loyalty
Being consistent
In everything you do
Proverbs 28:20

The fruit of GENTLENESS
Brings humility
It is quiet and gentle
Being loving
With tenderness and calm
Psalm 18:35

The fruit of KINDNESS
Being friendly
Being generous
Being considerate
Ephesians 4:32

The fruit of SELF-CONTROL
Being able to control
Emotions and desires
Creating positive behavior
2 Timothy 1:7

Galatians 5:22-23
"But the fruit of the Spirit is love, joy, peace,
patience, kindness, goodness, faithfulness,
gentleness, self-control; against such things
there is no law."

Happy Birthday Jesus

A little child
A little boy
Brought to earth
For such a time

A glorious light
Upon Him
The chosen one
The chosen King
The anointed one

Who one day
Is to be the King
To be the savior
The deliverer
The healer
For the nations

Others may despise Him
Others may embrace Him
The joy to the world
The prince of peace
The salvation of all

How grateful we are
To celebrate
The birth of this child
He is the greatest gift
Above all gifts
Baby Jesus

College

Many are called but
Few are chosen

Being in school
Ain't really cool
But after all it's
Your survival tool

People drop out
People take breaks
But returning is a challenge

Education wasn't on my mind
But God had me in His mind
To succeed is through education
But I don't want to pay attention
It wasn't really my intention
So help me Lord to be a representation
To the nation
Of the young generation

College is expensive
So are the bills
School and work
Is all I do
When will I be free?
Freedom is also a price
But God paid the price
With God all things are possible
Now I know nothing is impossible

May 9, 2020

This day, this date
The date of remembrance
Only few would understand
Only few would believe
This is the date
I would remember
A date that Heaven recorded
I am grateful
I am honored
Believing in such a miracle
A date to celebrate
A date to give thanks
I, myself couldn't believe it
Celebrating a graduate
Giving thanks to Almighty God
Honoring my spiritual parents for being there
I am a college graduate
I am a living testimony
Without God, I wouldn't be here
Without my spiritual parents,
I wouldn't have made it
Thank you for everything
Glory and honor to God

For Her

Someone who listens
Someone who understands
Someone who loves
With all her heart
Gives with all her heart
Protects with all her heart

A special friend
A special mother
A special teacher

The world admires you
The children admire you
Everyone admires you

You are the best
You do the best
In everything
You set your mind to

I love you
They love you
We love you

Thank you for all you've done
Thank you for teaching
Thank you for being there

Through the Storms

We are like the disciples
In the boat
Sailing through
To the final destination
Of where God wants us to be

We're all aiming
For one thing
In different callings
To what God wants

But through the mist
There are trials
There are tribulations
There are storms
Heading our way

Each person is unique
In their own way
In their own mind
In their own thoughts

Others have faith
Others need proof
Others just lack

Then we forget
Who was there,

Who came in,
Who never left

This is the moment
The moment of tests
The moment of trials

As the storm approaches
Closer and closer
Hearts beat faster
Bodies shaking

Did we forget
The one and only
Who is in the boat
Who came in the boat
Who sailed with us

Through the storms
He will be there
Through good times
He will be there
Through everything
He is there

Jesus sailed with us
Jesus was in the storm
Jesus is the peace
Through it all

Through the storm
Jesus reminds us
We have dominion
Over the seas
We have authority
To stop the storm

Believe it
Speak it
Overcome it

Speak peace
Speak life
Speak faith

Let's remember
Jesus is the peace
Jesus is the life
Jesus is here

Matthew 8:23-27

Butterfly

Life is like a butterfly
It has its season
It has its reason
There is timing for every season
There is timing for that reason
Enjoy the moment it gives
Enjoy the blessings it brings
There will be challenges
Keep the hopes
Hold on to the good memories
Let go of the bad memories
Embrace the present
Look forward to the future
You'll realize how far you've come
Wait patiently for the new changes
Don't let go, keep holding on
Don't fear but have faith
Time will come when you'll reach the sky
So be grateful
So be thankful
One day, you'll see the beauty
The beauty of life
Life will soon disappear like
The butterfly flying away

Resurrection

I once thought my life was over
Every being of me
I thought was over

My life seemed useless
My body has no being in it
It was an empty body
Already dissolving away
Feeling like life is useless

The dreams I had
Were drained from me
The faith I had
Had disappeared

The living being
Is no longer being
The desires also disappeared
Everything was gone

It was gone
It had disappeared
It had vanished
It was life that
Became lifeless

But…
One day

Jesus rose from the dead
So you and I could live
We don't have to die
If we receive His eternal life

Many of these had died
Hopes, dreams, desires, faith
But God resurrected it all
He entered my life

I believed in Him
I accepted Him
I received Him
Into my life
To become His life

Believing makes the dead of everything
Rise again

It's like a new song
A new human being
That rose within me
That came back to life

It was a revival within me

A new rebirth within me
A new resurrection within me
Of Jesus Christ

All the things
That had gone from me
Have become alive again

My dreams resurrected
My faith resurrected
My desires resurrected
My hope resurrected
I became a new
Resurrection

I received life
The eternal life
Through Jesus